Dea

Tre...
the best of all!

Tessa x

Text and illustration copyright ©2024 Tessa Venuti Sanderson
Published by Castenetto & Co
All rights reserved.

No part of this book may be produced in any form without
permission from the publisher.

Library of Congress cataloguing-in-publication data available.
ISBN 978-0-9933751-4-9
Printed by KDP.
Layout and design: Emy Farella

Ruby Luna's
Odyssey

TESSA VENUTI SANDERSON

For all young people.

Ruby Luna's mum wrote the words in this book for her. Ruby Luna decided to share it with you because sometimes it's easier to hear things about bodies from someone else's mum. It can feel less awkward.

You can read it in one go. You can read it one page at a time. There might be some parts that you read again and again while you let it sink in.

The pictures in the book are to remind you that lovely sensations in the body can come from everyday things. There's no rush to explore your body. Take your time.

Ruby Luna's mum wrote these words because it can take time to figure out all this stuff by yourself. Books can have an overwhelming amount of words in and searching the internet can show you things you didn't really want to see.

This is a private journey that only you can make. And you can talk to people about it. They'll have gone on this journey of discovery too. Even if you can't imagine it!

Your body is changing.
The changes can feel scary.
Or exciting. Or something else.

Your physical body helps you
to be in the world:
to move around,
to have different experiences.

From when your body
starts changing; from
a child's body to
an adult's body can take
10 whole years.

You might start
changing at 8 years or 10
or another time.
Your normal can be different
from someone else's normal.

Sometimes it can seem like
you're in a new place
without a map.

Without a map

How are you meant to
navigate this body
when it looks different,
feels different, even
smells different than before?

Your body is changing.
The changes might be annoying.
Or make you very curious.
Or feel something else.

Being in a body
provides all sorts of sensations:
heaviness
itchiness
pins and needles
cramps
growing pains
aches
restless legs
shivering

butterflies in your tummy
breathing fast
breathing slowly
feeling sleepy
warm cosiness
snug as a bug in a rug
light-headed
giddy with excitement
or bursting with energy.

Physical sensations
can start to change too.
You might feel tingling
or warmth in your body
without knowing why.

This might be concentrated
around private parts of the body
like the breasts or vulva,
or you may be sensitive
somewhere else: your ears,
your feet, your back.
Or you might not.

We can enjoy the sensations
in our body from everyday things:
like the feeling of water
on your skin in the shower,
the warmth of sun on your face,
the coolness of a breeze

Butterflies in your tummy

on your arms on a hot day,
the softness of a blanket,
the juiciness of a ripe peach
exploding with sweetness in your mouth,
the heaviness of a big blanket in winter,
the rumbling of your stomach when
you know your favourite meal is ready,
the glow from a belly laugh.

When you start to become aware
of your body as a source of pleasure
all by itself
it might be confusing.

Depending on the messages
you picked up from social media,
your teachers, your friends,
your family...
you might feel that it's not right
to feel pleasure in your body.
You might even feel ashamed.

There is nothing to be
ashamed about. Truly.

When you realise that
parts of your body are
somehow different than others,
it can feel awkward.

When you realise that
people react to your body
and you maybe react to
others' bodies,
it can feel alarming,
strange, exciting
or something else.

Can you see your body as
an incredible vehicle or vessel
to take you through life
to have adventures?

Suddenly you might be aware
of bodies all around you.
Bodies that look the same.
Bodies that look different.

Exciting feelings

On social media, TV, Netflix,
gaming: the same body type
seems to be everywhere.
The effortlessly perfect body.

It's a myth.

The bodies you see are
filtered,
scooped in,
taped up,
sucked in,
body shaping
underwear put on,
professionally styled.

They might be hungry bodies.
Photographed from the
most flattering angle,
on a good day, in good lighting,
not when having belly bloating
or a breakout of acne.

Knowing all this
won't affect the
scrutiny you feel,
but perhaps you'll
be able to judge
yourself less.
View yourself with
kind eyes, just like
you see your friends.

Look around you at real bodies:
Your friends, teachers,
Parents, friends' parents,
grandparents,
neighbours.
Look at the diversity of bodies.

All bodies can feel
pleasure, not only
the seemingly
effortlessly
perfect
ones.

Different bodies

The body changes most
through puberty
but the truth is
it keeps on changing.

Your body at 25
will be like a
different land
compared to your
body at 15.

Over your lifetime,
it might change through
exercise or healthy eating,
stress or illness,
hormonal contraception,
pregnancy and birth,
perimenopause,
menopause
when your periods stop,
and old age.

It can be hard to
get used to having
periods.
Especially if they're
heavy or make
you feel faint.

While you get used to your
changing body
it might be hard to believe
that when you are older
you will likely miss the body
you have now.
Or think how incredible
it actually was.

Different ages

Back to pleasure and finding
pleasure in your own body...

Sensitive areas to touch
are where nerve endings
are plentiful.
The lips, tongue,
fingers, toes,
nipples,
vulva,
clitoris.

The skin all over your body
can be sensitive to touch.
Loving touch is
healthy.

You do you.
Explore what feels good to you.
It might change later.
You don't have to decide now and
then it's fixed in stone.

If you know what you like,
one day you can share that with
someone else if you want to.

And they can share what sensations
they find pleasurable for their body.
Then you can decide if you want
to explore each other's body.
Or not.

Sharing touch
based on trust
and respect
is wonderful.

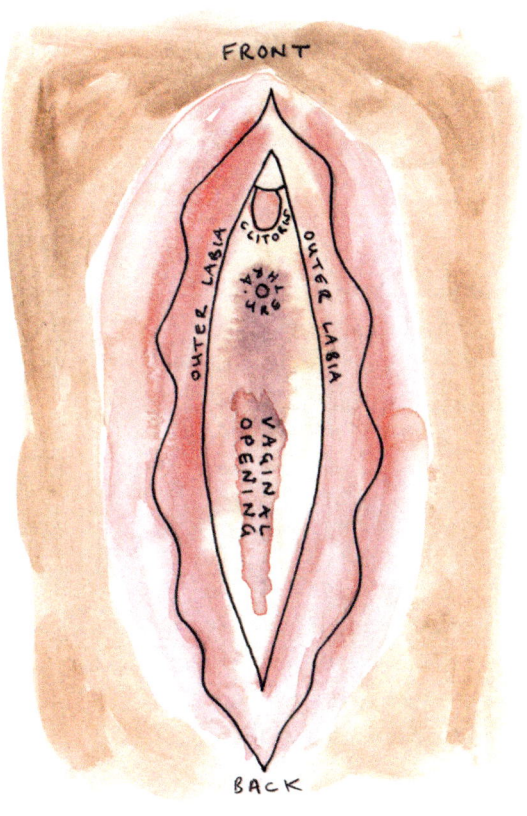

You might feel strong feelings
of attraction
or hotness
or lust.

Perhaps you feel like you cannot
satisfy those feelings alone.
But can you explore what sensations
feel warm, exciting, fantastic
in your own body?

A physical relationship is a bit like
if you want to make your favourite meal:
you think about what ingredients
are needed to make it just right.

If someone makes your
favourite meal
they will ask you what it is you want.
What combination of foods
will make you happy.

If they've never made it before
they will need to ask you
and keep checking with you
if they're doing it right.

Sex. What happens when
you hear that word?
Do you cringe, feel embarrassed,
Awkward or shrink to make
yourself smaller?
Or are you super curious?
All of these are normal reactions.

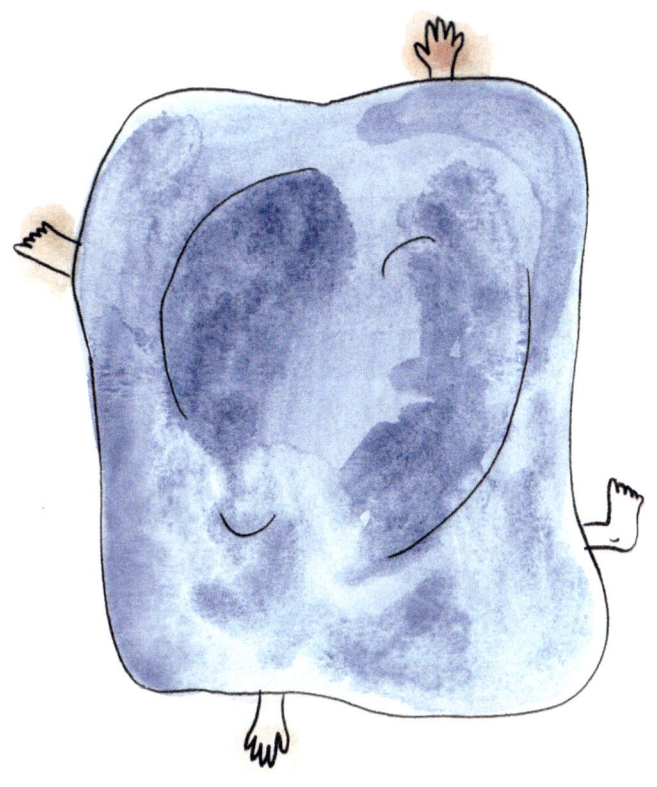

What is sex?

Sex education at school.
Too much information?
Too little information?
Different people will
feel differently.

Sometimes young people
(and some adults!)
think sex is what happens in
porn.

What is this porn thing
that sex ed warns you about?
Pornography is made
to stimulate
sexual excitement.

Porn is made to get a quick reaction.
It displays genitals
and sexual activity in an
intense and dramatic way.

Once you see these things
you can't unsee them.
It can also be addictive.

Porn often shows extreme
sexual activity and makes it
seem normal and seem like
everyone is enjoying it.

Porn can be addictive
because people need
more and more intensity
to get the same reaction.

It's a bit like eating
really spicy crisps
until you can't taste
the hotness anymore
so you try an even
spicier flavour.
Except on a whole
other level.
Obviously.

Seeing things
you can't unsee

Seeing porn can make
people want to act
out extreme things.
Or they become
numb
to everyday pleasure
and real intimacy.

Porn isn't real life.
A lot of what happens in porn
is not healthy.
It is made for views
and money, not your
pleasure.

Sex is not only about
putting body parts inside
other body parts!
Intimacy can be kissing
and stroking
and hugging.
You decide what
you want.
When and if
you're ready.

If you don't want
to do something,
being made to feel
bad about it
is not ok.

The legal age for
sexual activity
is sixteen.
You can wait until
you're a bit older
or much older.
When YOU are ready.

You're not frigid,
or cold, or immature
if you don't want to.
Or if you don't feel
those sensations,
don't have the desire.

Or not found the
right person to feel
comfortable enough.
Or to make it special.

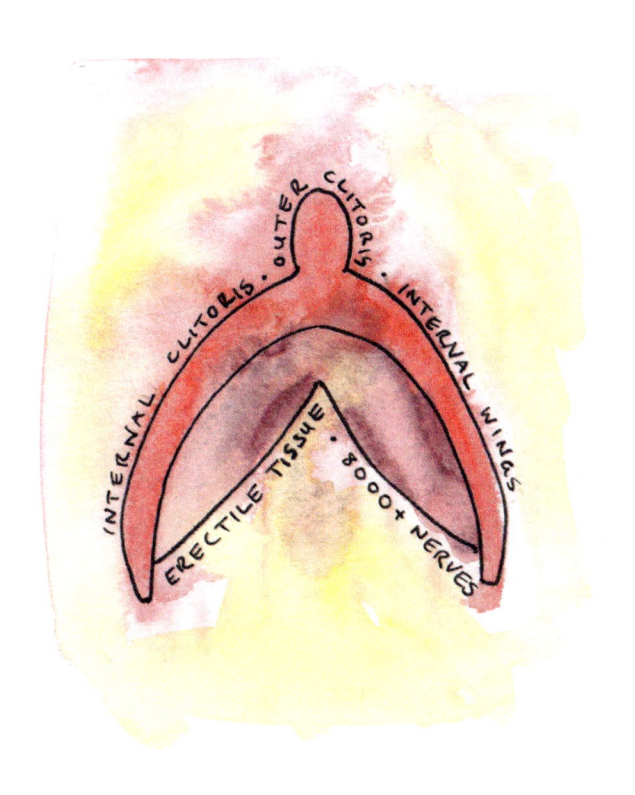

Wings of the clitoris

For female bodies,
pleasure builds slowly.

Female bodies have
erectile tissue:
in the tip of the clitoris
and the wings of
the clitoris
either side of the
vaginal opening.

For this to feel pleasurable
needs a feeling of safety
and time to build.

With TikTok
and YouTube shorts
we laugh quickly
or swipe on.

When you pause
for a moment
and really feel
a sensation,
pleasure can be quick.

Being in your onesie,
holding a cup of
hot chocolate in your hands,
splashing in a puddle
even if you have your school
shoes on and you're not
meant to,
making someone laugh.

Pleasure in a cup!

When it comes to bodies,
it might take more time.
To make friends with your
changing body:
to understand her,
to accept her.

Exploring your body is ok.
In fact, it's great.
In your bedroom
with privacy.
Explain that you want
people to knock
before they come in
from now on.

You can use a mirror
to see what you look like.
The vulva changes as
your body changes.

Just like bodies look different
vulvas look different.
The labia – lips of the vulva –
may start to show more.
Totally normal.

Just like breasts, the labia
might be different
each side.
Totally normal.

The internet can take you
down all sorts of rabbit holes
if you try to search for words
like sex, vulva, labia, breasts.

Breasts vary

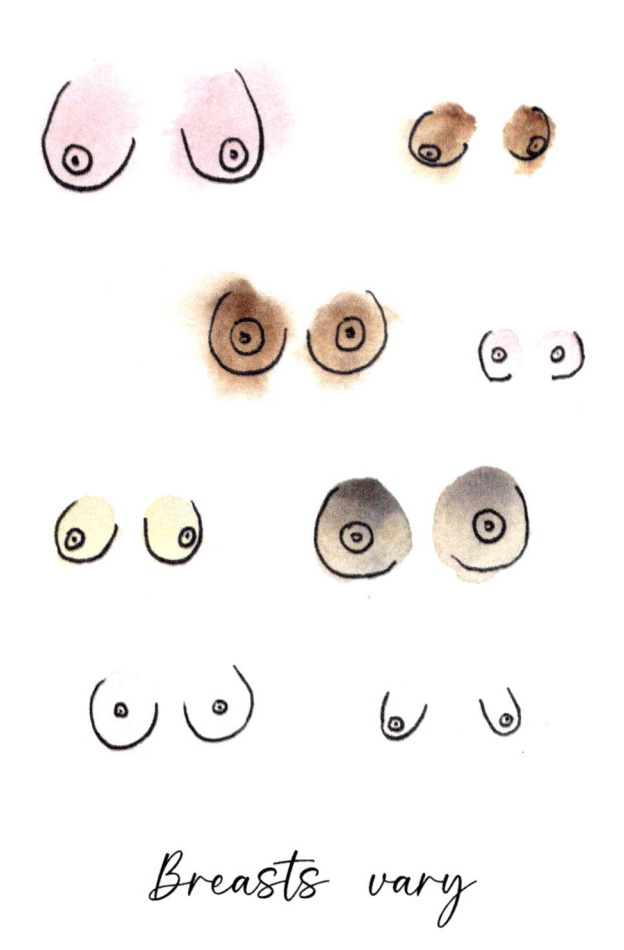

Ask a parent, a teacher, a friend
if they have a book they can
lend you instead.

Your parents went through puberty.
I know it's hard to imagine.
And it was different then.
They might find it hard to talk about
your body changing,
but less so if they gave you this book.

You can ask them about stuff
when they're driving somewhere
looking at the traffic and not you.
Don't give up if they don't answer
properly the first time.
They might have been surprised.

Maybe their parents didn't explain
things to them very well
and it will take them time to
find the right words.

Be kind to yourself too.
Your changing female body
is a big deal.

If your body gives you
difficult feelings
tell someone.
To share your feelings
might be enough.

The feelings might feel
too big to handle.
Asking for help
to find a counsellor
who works with young people
can change your life.

Ask questions
in the car

You are worth listening to.
How you feel matters.

When you feel that
you matter,
your pleasure in life
and in your body
will soar.

Imagine how it feels
when you make someone laugh.
The exhilaration and
Expansiveness.
Your unique body can make
you feel like that.

It might take a
while to figure it out.
That's ok.

Self-care through the month,
not just during your period
is great.
From a cosy blanket,
to a hot water bottle,
a bath or your
favourite meal.

You do you.
Know your own body.
Be the queen of your own body.
Don't settle for anything less.
You do you.

Be your own queen

The end

What I like most about my body is...

Everyday sensations I enjoy are...
(e.g. sun on my face, water on my skin)

In the shower

The weirdest thing about puberty is...

At school, sex education was...

The people I can talk to about my feelings are...

Big feelings

When I start comparing myself to others, I can...

(e.g. turn off my phone and put music on, chat with a friend, look at photos of me as a kid – so cute!)

The things that make me feel loved are...

(e.g. when my favourite meal is made for me, when my PE kit is already packed when I'm rushing in the morning)

To look after myself, I can...
(e.g. do a short yoga video, have a warm bath)

Cosy in a blanket

Resources page

You can get support from...

https://www.childline.org.uk/ - online or phone

https://www.youngminds.org.uk/ - information and advice on mental health

https://teenagehelpline.org.uk/ - 24/7 helpline for teens

https://sexedrescue.com/ - sex education information for parents and children

https://www.amazingme.com.au/ - sexual health education for parents to know how to support you

See Tessa's other books:

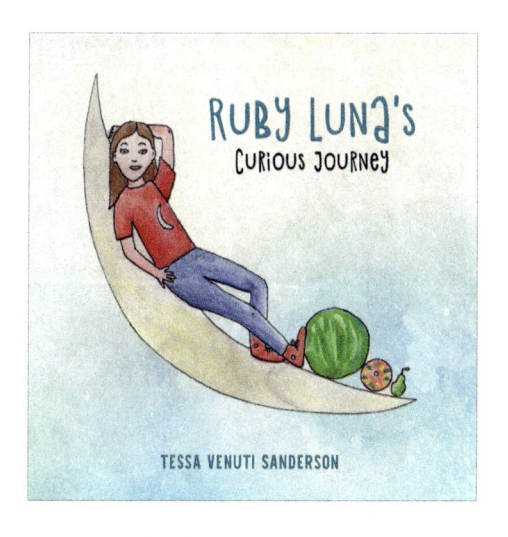

Ruby Luna's Curious Journey
(5+ years)

Go with Ruby Luna on a journey around her body finding out the correct words to speak about her lower anatomy and discovering what is where. The book helps support parents to answer those tricky questions and has multicultural, relatable illustrations and fun actions to keep it entertaining. Aimed at 5-10 year olds girls.

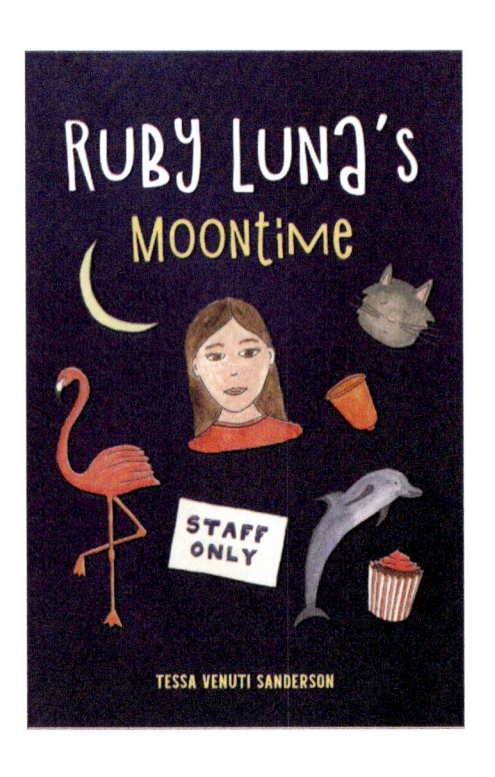

Ruby Luna's Moontime
(8+ years)

Ruby Luna has something exciting happen to her. She can't wait to tell her half-sister and friends. She's the first one in her class and there's a lot to think about when you get your period! A fun, informative novella written in diary format.

Colour Your Cycle:
INNER SEASON MANDALAS

17 hand-drawn mandalas to reflect on the gifts and tasks of the inner seasons of the menstrual cycle, with stories, insights and a yoga nidra relaxation.

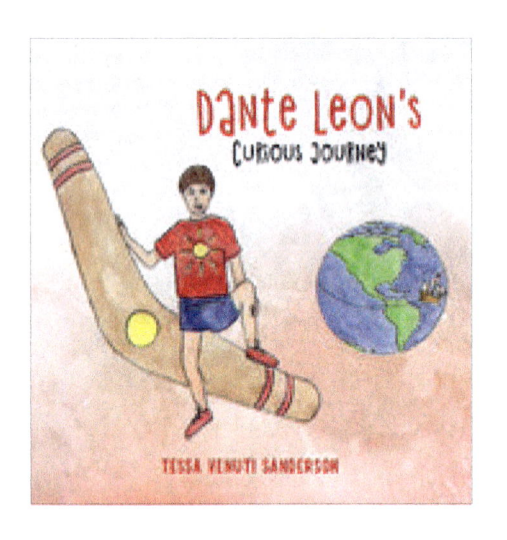

Dante Leon's Curious Journey
(7+ years)

Follow Dante Leon and his friends on a journey around the male body and how it changes during puberty. In a similar format to Ruby Luna's Curious Journey, the multi-cultural and fun drawings, and crazy facts keep children entertained. Aimed at 7-11 year old boys.